Why Bears Have Short Tails

Written by Hiawyn Oram

Illustrated by Beccy Blake

Harcourt
Supplemental Publishers

Rigby • Steck-Vaughn

www.steck-vaughn.com

Long ago, Bear was not like he is today.
Back then, he had a long tail.
Back then, he was always hungry.
Then a long, hard winter came.

It got cold.
Then it got colder.
The river turned to ice.
Bear could not fish.

All the animals were hungry—
well, almost all the animals.

Fox was never hungry.
He always had fish.
He always had big fish and little fish.
He always had long fish and short fish.

One day, Fox went out to fish.

Bear went to Fox's home.

He stole a big fish.

The big fish was good.

The next day, Bear went back.
He stole a little fish.
Bear was about to eat the little fish
when Fox came back!

Bear said, "Fox, I am very sorry.
I want to change.
Teach me to fish under the ice.
Then I will never steal your fish again."

Fox asked, "Teach you?
Oh, yes, Bear.
I will teach you, and you will change."

Bear and Fox went to the river.
Fox made a hole in the ice.
He said, "Put your tail in the hole.
You will feel the fish pulling your tail."
Bear put his long tail in the hole.

Fox asked, "Can you feel the fish pulling?"
Bear said, "Yes, I can!
They are pulling hard.
I am catching some fish!
Can I pull up my tail now?"

FOX'S TOOLS

Fox said, "Oh, no!
It is not time.
Keep fishing.
I will come back soon."

But Fox did not come back soon.
He did not come back for a long time.
Bear could feel the fish pulling his tail.
He said, "It must be time now.
I will pull up my tail."

Bear pulled.

His tail would not come out of the river.

Bear pulled hard.

He pulled so hard that his tail came off!

It was frozen in the ice!

Fox came back.

He laughed, "Ha! Ha! Ha!

I said you would change, and you did!

Fish were not pulling on your tail.

The river was freezing it.

Never steal my fish again!"

Bear was very sorry.

That winter changed him forever.

Today, all bears have short tails.

And they never feel hungry in winter!